A Walk in the Woods

Written by
Kurt Bigbee

Illustrated by
Nori Kimura

A Walk in the Woods
Copyright © 2019 by Kurt Bigbee

All rights reserved. No part of this publication may be reproduced, stored in a retrieval system, or transmitted by any means – electronic, mechanical, photographic (photocopying), recording, or otherwise – without prior permission in writing from the author.

Printed in the United States of America
ISBN-13: 978-1-944483-28-9 (GreenTree Publishers)

GreenTree Publishers
www.greentreepublishers.com

Dedication and Special Thanks

Dedicated to young and old children everywhere, with the hope that caring for this planet brings joy to them & future generations.

Thanks Kama, Nori, Tim, Pauline, Ann, Sara, Jerald, Jo and so many others for your dedication, patience and helpful comments.

Zeke and Riley were quietly amazed as they went for a walk with Mommy in the woods.

Their feet left faint footprints in the spongy earth. The mist was still clearing, but rays of sunlight pierced through here and there, reaching out for the green leaves and brown trunks.

The morning's silence was broken by a distant buzzing noise, like the dirt bikes that raced by the house some days. The buzz was followed by silence, then a loud creaking, and a crash as something huge fell to the ground.

"What was that noise?" exclaimed Riley.

"It sounded like T-rex!" Zeke responded.

Mommy knew loggers would be in the area, so she led the children to a hill high above the danger zone, far away from the falling trees. From a safe location, they observed the clearing that had been recently harvested.

"Ugh," said Zeke. "Looks like a battlefield." He was staring at the piles of debris scattered around the valley. It reminded him of the war-torn cities he had seen on TV.

"Looks like a graveyard to me," said Riley. She pointed to the tree stumps standing like tombstones, all that remained of the living trees that had shaded the clearing not too long ago.

That's ugly, Mom," she said. "The people that did this are mean!"

"Not necessarily," Mommy replied. "It depends on how they treat the land when they are done. Let's take a closer look far away from the loggers. We can also visit this clearing in the future, to see whether people tending this land are just being mean or if they are good stewards."

"What's a steward?" asked Zeke.

"A steward is like a babysitter, or a gardener," answered Mommy. "They take care of the land and forest. If they 'cut and run', meaning they just leave it like this, they might be considered mean or irresponsible. However, if they observe proper cutting rules, clear the land and replant, they are probably good stewards. Like a farmer. "

"What does it mean to observe proper cutting rules?" Zeke asked.

"There are several ways to properly cut trees from a forest," Mommy explained. "A proper cutting rule starts by leaving enough trees to naturally drop seeds or planting new trees if there aren't enough left standing. Let's keep walking and see how they are caring for the woods."

The threesome ventured into an open, sunlit area, and began exploring. Zeke hopped from stump to stump and pulled his foot back just in time to avoid stepping on a small tree.

Mommy explained that this small tree was called a seedling. It was no taller than his hand with branches as thin as toothpicks.

Zeke reached out and felt the soft needles of the branch in his hand. "It's like a bottle brush, only softer!" he exclaimed.

Riley was bending over another seedling, and Mommy knelt beside a third. He gazed around the area and was surprised to see dozens of seedlings all planted at a distance about the length of the minivan Mommy drove to school each morning.

"They're all over!" Zeke cried. "These people must be good stewards after all."

"You're getting the idea," said Mommy, "but let's look around for other signs."

They walked along in the warm sun that had now burnt off most of the mist. Birds chirped from the short grasses, and occasionally a slight breeze would lift their hair and let it fall again.

The clearing had been cleaned up by loggers, so the walk was not too difficult. Before long, they heard a brook babbling in the distance. The morning air was warming up. Splashing in the water sounded like fun!

Back into the woods they marched, picking up their pace in the cool shade. It was several minutes before they reached the brook, and it was worth the short hike. The water was clear and inviting.

Zeke picked up a flat stone and tried skipping it in shallow water. Taking off their shoes, they waded onto smooth stones and reached down to splash water on their faces. Before long, they were splashing water at each other.

Zeke wiped off droplets of water hanging from his eyelashes and chin. "Why didn't they cut down the trees between the clearing and the brook?" he asked.

"Good question," answered Mommy. "Riley, do you know why?"

"Is it because they're good stewards?" asked Riley.

"Very good!" said Mommy. "The trees between the clearing and the brook are called the buffer zone, and they protect the water. The tree roots keep the soil from washing away, so the water is clean. Shade from the tall trees helps the water stay cool for fish and other creatures."

They put on their shoes, crossed the brook on a solid log, and resumed their walk. Zeke and Riley had to balance carefully with every step, or they might be swimming in the water with the fish!

Soon they reached an open area with plenty of sun and trees as tall as their Mommy.

"This is a young forest, "said Mommy, "and these young trees are called saplings. They're about fifteen years old."

"It sure takes time to grow a forest!" said Riley.

"Yes, it does," agreed Mommy, "but all good things take time. When people harvest a forest, they need to steward or take care of the land, so it will grow new trees. It's similar to raising young children—they need food, water, sunshine, and encouragement—all the things to help them grow. In some ways, it is just like growing people."

Riley and Zeke had a fun walk in the woods, but now it was time to go home.

"I want to be a good steward of the forest when I grow up," Riley said.

"Me, too," Zeke agreed.

"You don't have to wait until you're a grownup," Mommy said. "You can start right now by planting trees and helping to take care of the forest."

The two children smiled up at their mother as they headed toward home. They knew they had learned some valuable lessons about stewardship that could be practiced for the rest of their lives.

US Forest Service Tree Planting Statistics

1) There were 96.6 billion trees counted in the 2016 survey.

2) Trees outnumber people by 300 to 1.

3) The National Forest Foundation plans to plant 50 million trees.

4) The National Arbor Day Foundation has planted 60 million trees over 26 years.

Plant a tree! Check with local or state government or environmental organizations for tree resources. Before planting a tree, be sure it's a good match for the planting location.

Things to do on your own.

Draw a line between the number and when it occurred in the story.

1

2

3

4

This picture shows trees of different ages. Draw a picture for each stage of a tree.

Seedling

Sapling

Adult tree

Find the animals in the picture below: 1 - chickadee, 1 - Squirrel, 1 - Rabbit, 1 - doe, and 2 – fawns.

Count the fish in the drawing below.

Draw a fish!

Made in the USA
Lexington, KY
03 November 2019